Faraal Foods...
for fasting days

Tarla Dalal
INDIA'S #1 COOKERY AUTHOR

S&C
SANJAY & CO.
MUMBAI

First Printing : 2010

ISBN : 978-93-80392-02-8

Copyright © Sanjay & Co.

"Tarla Dalal" is also a registered trademark owned by Sanjay & Co.

All rights reserved with the publishers.

No part of this book may be reproduced, stored in a retrieval system or transmitted by any means, electronic, mechanical, photocopying, recording or otherwise, without the written permission of the publishers.

DISCLAIMER : While every precaution has been taken in the preparation of this book, the publishers and the author assume no responsibility for errors or omissions. Neither is any liability assumed for damages resulting from the use of information contained herein.

Price: Rs. 99/-

Published & Distributed by : **Sanjay & Company**

353/ A-1, Shah & Nahar Industrial Estate, Dhanraj Mill Compound, Lower Parel (W), Mumbai - 400 013. INDIA.
Tel. : (91-22) 4345 2400 • Fax : (91-22) 2496 5876 • E-mail : sanjay@tarladalal.com • Website : www.tarladalal.com

Printed by : Minal Sales Agencies, Mumbai

UK and USA customers can call us on :

UK : 02080029533   •   USA : 213-634-1406

For books, Membership on **tarladalal.com**, Subscription for **Cooking & More** and Recipe queries

Timing : 9.30 a.m. to 7.00 p.m. (IST), from Monday to Saturday

Local call charges applicable

Recipe Research & Food Styling : Nisha Katira Brinda Gandhi	**Designed by :** Vinod Patil	**Photography :** Sanjay Dalal - page 13, 23, 31, 42, 48, 53, 54, 59, 65, 66, 70, 77, 79, 81, 83, 85 and 89 Nirav Mehta - page 29, 32, 36, 60, 75 and 87
	Typesetting : Adityas Enterprises	**Copy Editing :** Janani Gopalakrishnan Vikram

BULK PURCHASES : Tarla Dalal Cookbooks are ideal gifts. If you are interested in buying more than 500 assorted copies of Tarla Dalal Cookbooks at special prices, please contact us at 91-22-4345 2400 or email : sanjay@tarladalal.com

INTRODUCTION

The word fasting brings to our mind *sabudana wada*, *doodhi ka halwa* and hot *faraali pattice*. Yes, this has been a part of the traditional meal for fasting days. But have you ever thought of relishing *pakodas, idli-sambhar, misal* and so on during fasts? My this book on **"Faraal Foods"** is an attempt to demystify the world of *faraal* foods with newer recipes to be enjoyed by one and all on fasting days.

This book offers a fabulous variety of recipes with something for every food lover depending on their tastes and preferences, from savoury combos to amazingly rich sweets. **33 recipes have been divided into 5 major sections viz. Drinks, Snacks, Main Course, Accompaniments and Desserts.** My diet–conscious readers will also be happy to note that I have not forgotten them. Many of the recipes like **Healthy Wafer Platter, page 27, Upvaas Thalipeeth, page 51, Faraali Dosa, page 73** are some healthy alternatives to fat-laden ingredients, to help cut down on the recipe's calorie count.

The book also provides you an insight on the most common ingredients allowed during fasts along with their names in regional languages for your easy reference. Although you are sure to notice same ingredients are used to cook many recipes, but believe me the end-result of each recipe is distinctly different and delicious.

Hope you enjoy this novel offering of mine and may you make your way to everybody's heart, through their stomach with this innovative *faraal* recipes.

Regards,

Tarla Dalal

INDEX

Drinks

Main Course

Snacks

Accompniments

Desserts

Basic Recipe

Where abouts of Fasting

Fasting is the act of willingly abstaining oneself from some or all foods, drinks or both, for a selected period of time.

Fasting is done for religious and spiritual reasons and is mentioned in the Bible, in old and New Testament, the Quran, the Mahabharata and the Upanishads. It is done to gain good deeds and to impress different Deities and Gods. Fasting also teaches self-control and self– regulatory way of functioning and also helps the body to gain back its vitality.

Some Hindus fast on certain days of the month such as *Ekadasi* or *Purnima*, and also certain days of the week are also set-aside for fasts depending on personal belief and favourite deity. For example, devotees of Lord Shiva tend to fast on Mondays, while Devotees of Vishnu tend to fast on Fridays or Saturdays, devotees of Lord Ganesh fast on Tuesdays and specials days like *Shankhasti* and *Chathurthi*.

Fasting during religious festivals is also very common in a diverse country like India. Some examples are *Mahashivratri*, here most people conduct a fast by consuming only fruits and milk, *Navratri*, the 9 days of fast, which occurs twice in a year.

Unlike the strict fasts like *Paryushan*, kept by Jains and *Roza* kept by the Muslims, Hindu fasts are relatively lenient and there are an array of ingredients permitted during these fasts.

Some of the ingredients that find prominence in a fasting household are:

FOOD GROUP	INGREDIENTS ALLOWED
CEREALS	Sago (*sabudana*), buckwheat (*kutto/ kutto no daro*), buckwheat (*kutto/ kutto no daro*) flour, waterchestnut *(singhada)* flour, whole *rajgira* seeds is consumed in form of *rajgira chikki* on fasting days, *rajgira* flour, arrowroot *(paniphal)* flour and sanwa millet *(sama)* and its flour.
VEGETABLES	Potatoes, puple yam (*kand*), yam (*suran*), sweet potato (*shakarkand*), bottle gourd (*doodhi/ lauki*)*, cucumber*, carrots*, lemon. Leafy vegetables like fresh coriander (*dhania*)* and mint leaves (*phudina*)*.
FRUITS	All fruits are permitted (except in some fasts like *Santoshi Mata* fasts where citrus or sour fruits are abstained from consuming).
SPICES	Coriander (*dhania*)*, cumin seeds (*jeera*), curry leaves (*kadi patta*)*, ginger (*adrak*), dry ginger (*soonth*), dry ginger (*soonth*) powder, green chillies, tamarind (*imli*), lemon, round red chillies (*boriya mirchi*)*, round red chilli (*boryia mirchi*) powder*, red chillies*, red chilli powder* and coconut and poppy seeds (*khus–khus*).
DAIRY PRODUCTS	Milk and its products like curds (*dahi*), *paneer* (cottage cheese), ghee, white butter *(makhan)* and cream.
NUTS AND OIL SEEDS	Almonds (*badam*), cashewnuts (*kaju*), pistachios, walnuts (*akhrot*), raisins, lotus seeds (*makhane*) and peanuts.
MISCELLANEOUS	Readymade sweets strictly made from nuts and oilseeds, dairy products and coconut.

* These ingredients are consumed by some communities while avoided by others.

Insight into Main Ingredients for Faraal

Sago (sabudana)

Sago is used in Indian cooking, especially as a light-meal choice for *Ekadasi* / fasting days. Sago is a powdery starch made from the processed pith found inside the trunks of the sago palm. It comes in different sizes - small, medium and large, buy accordingly. Avoid if yellowish tint or creamish colour is seen on the grains.

Every grain of sago has to be separate, hence it's essential that you don't over-soak it, or it will turn out like a sticky paste. When cooked they turn from their opaque white color to translucent, and become soft and spongy.

Rajgira Four

Rajgira flour is obtained from *Rajgira* / Ramadana which is the seed of the amaranth plant. It has a very little pale cream colour and a fine texture. When strictly non – cereal items are required in India during specific fasting days, this one fits a bit nicely.

Sanwa Millet (sama) and its flour

Sanwa millet is tasteless, creamish in colour, more granulated and bigger than semolina *(rawa)*. The fact that is found wild when harvested, and that it is "cooling" for the body, makes it a viable choice during days of fasting. Though sanwa millet *(sama)* flour is not easily available in the market, it can be made at home by grinding the sanwa millet *(sama)* into fine textured flour or coarsely ground flour as per the recipe requirements.

Waterchestnut (singhada) flour

Waterchestnut *(singhada)* flour is made from dried waterchestnuts. It is tasteless and white in colour and

has a very fine texture. The waterchestnuts are boiled, peeled, processed and then ground into flour. The flour is then used to make *chapatis*, *parathas*, sweets, *wadas* and also as a binding or thickening agent.

Buckwheat *(kutto/ kutti no daro)* and its flour

Buckwheat is a plant crop and is cultivated mainly for its grains. Buckwheat is sold whole or in cracked form and is usually brown in colour. It has a distinctive nutty flavour.

Though buckwheat flour is not easily available in the market, buckwheat flour can also be made at home by grinding the broken buckwheat or whole buckwheat gorths that are easily available in the market, into fine textured flour or coarsely ground flour as per recipe requirement.

Arrowroot *(paniphal)* flour

Arrowroot flour is ground from the dried roots of the *Marantha* plant and is very useful as a thickener and as a binding agent. This fine whitish flour is tasteless, and becomes clear when it is cooked, but emits a faint odour when mixed with boiling water. It has a very fine texture.

Rock salt *(sendha namak)*

Rock salt is the mineral form of sodium chloride, commonly known as sendha *namak* in India. The mineral is typically colorless to yellow. The rock salt is derived from the salt mountains. The rock salt occurs in vast beds of sedimentary evaporite minerals that result from the drying up of enclosed lakes and seas. Salt beds may be up to hundreds of meters thick and underlie broad areas.

It is commonly used as a condiment and food preservative. A large amount of the commercially mined rock salt is prepared for human consumption, especially on fasting days. We have used rock salt in out recipes as in India, most communities use only rock salt to season their food on fasting days. **However you can consume table salt as per your religious beliefs.**

Regional Names of Common Faraal Foods

Here's a list of *faraal* foods in common Indian languages to the best of our knowledge.

Ingredients	Hindi	Marathi	Gujarati	Bengali	Tamil	Malayalam	Kannada	Oriya	Telugu
Sago	Sago	Sabudana	Sabudana	Saboo	Javvarish	Sago	Sabbakki	Sagudana	Saggu-biyyam
Rajgira Four	Ramda na atta	Rajigara pith	Rajagara no lott	–	–	–	–	–	–
Sanwa Millet	Shama/ Bhagar	Shamul/ Varai/ Bhagar	Moriyo/ Sama	Shamula	Samwa chawal/ Kundiraivalu	–	–	–	Bonta chamalu
Waterchestnut Flour	Singhara ka atta	Singhara cha pith	Shingoda no lott	Paniphal flour	Singhaha	Karimpolam atta	Samai	Panisin-ghara	Kubyakam
Buckwheat	Kottu	Kottu	Kutti no daro	–	Kootu	Kootu	–	–	–
Arrowroot Flour	Tikhor/ Paniphal	Toukil	Arrawrrot	Tavkeel	Kuva mavu	Koovapodi	Tavaksha	Araroot	
Rock salt	Sendha namak	Sendha mith	Sindhalu	–	–	–	–	–	–

Reference: Gopalan C., Rama Sastri B.V. & Balasubramanian S.C. (1995): Nutritive Value of Indian Foods.

Availability & Storage Tips

Generally all the ingredients are best used fresh. However it is common for everyone to buy batches of main ingredients used on *faraal* days and store at home.

Always store *faraal* ingredients in an air-tight containers in refrigerator. The refrigerator is a very good storage area for foods like buckwheat and its flour, *sanwa* millet and its flour, *rajgira* flour, waterchestnut flour, arrowroot floor. When refrigerated, the ingredients can stay fresh as long as 6 months. However sago is an exception and does not require refrigeration.

Do not mix the old and new stock. Keep it away from moisture, as little water can make the whole thing soggy thereby making it unacceptable for cooking.

Most of the ingredients and flours permitted are available only at the local grocery shops all around the year.

DRINKS
Piyush

Worthy of a festive day, this luxurious drink is drawn from Maharashtrian cuisine and is sure to amaze your taste buds!

Preparation Time: A few minutes.
Cooking Time: Nil.
Makes 4 glasses.

2 cups *kesar*-flavoured *shrikhand*, readily available in the market

3 cups fresh buttermilk

2 tbsp sugar

A pinch cardamom *(elaichi)* powder

A pinch nutmeg *(jaiphal)* powder

For the garnish

2 tbsp sliced pistachios

A few strands saffron *(kesar)*

1. Combine the *shrikhand*, buttermilk, sugar, cardamom powder and nutmeg powder in a bowl and whisk well.
2. Refrigerate for at least 2 hours.
3. Pour equal quantities of the drink in 4 individual glasses and serve chilled garnished with pistachios and saffron.

Thandai

A shaahi drink in which mild spices romance with almonds and milk resulting in a rich taste. Make the paste in advance and mix it with milk whenever hunger pangs strike on a fasting day.

Preparation Time: 5 minutes.
Cooking Time: 10 to 12 minutes.
Makes 6 glasses.

To blended into a *thandai* paste

¼ cup almonds *(badam)*, soaked, drained and peeled

2 tbsp fennel seeds *(saunf)*

10 to 12 peppercorns *(kalimirch)*

4 tsp poppy seeds *(khus -khus)*

2 pinches cardamom *(elaichi)* powder

A few strands saffron *(kesar)* dissolved in 1 tbsp warm milk

1 tbsp rose water

Other ingredients

5 cups milk

½ cup powdered sugar

For the garnish

A few chopped rose petals

1. Bring the milk to boil in a broad non-stick pan and cool completely.
2. Add the *thandai* paste and mix well.
3. Refrigerate for at least for 3 to 4 hours.
4. Strain using a strainer, add the sugar and mix well.
   Serve chilled garnished with rose petals.

Minty Mango Delight

A mint-laced mango drink that is just the right thing to boost your energy levels while you fast in the summer, when mangoes are aplenty!

Preparation Time: 10 minutes.
Cooking Time: 10 minutes.
Makes 4 glasses.

¼ cup sugar
1 cup peeled raw mangoes *(kairi)* cubes
6 to 8 mint leaves *(phudina)*
1 cup crushed ice

For the garnish
4 sprigs of mint leaves *(phudina)*

1. Combine the sugar with ½ cup of water in a saucepan, mix well and cook on a medium flame till the sugar dissolves, while stirring continuously.
2. Add the raw mangoes and cook on a medium flame till the mangoes are tender, while stirring twice in between. Keep aside to cool.
3. Combine the cooked mangoes and mint leaves and blend in a mixer till smooth.
4. In each glass, place ¼ cup of crushed ice and pour equal quantity of the drink over it.
   Serve immediately garnished with a mint sprig.

Angoor ka Sherbat

A simple yet delectable drink that is also visually-appealing, this is a beverage of black grapes perked up with lemon and ginger juices.

Preparation Time: 10 minutes.
Cooking Time: Nil.
Makes 4 glasses.

2 cups black or green grapes
1 tbsp powdered sugar
1 tsp cumin seeds *(jeera)* powder
2 tsp lemon juice
1 tsp ginger *(adrak)* juice

1. Combine the grapes with 3½ cups of water and blend in a mixer to a smooth purée.
2. Strain the purée through a sieve and add the sugar, cumin seeds powder, lemon juice and ginger juice and mix well. Refrigerate till chill.
3. Pour equal quantities of the drink into 4 individual glasses and serve chilled.

Coconut Kewra Drink

This unusual medley of tender coconut and readymade kewra syrup is truly irresistible. Take a drink break that is sure to refresh you so much that you will forget you are on a fast!

Preparation Time: A few minutes.
Cooking Time: Nil.
Makes 4 glasses.

4 cups coconut water
4 tbsp chopped tender coconut meat *(nariyal ki malai)*
4 tsp *kewra* syrup, readily available in the market
1 cup crushed ice

1. Combine all the ingredients, except the ice in a bowl, and mix well.
2. In each glass, place ¼ cup of crushed ice and pour equal quantities of the drink over it.
   Serve immediately.

SNACKS

Kand Aloo Pakoda

Enjoy these crispy peanut-flavoured pakodas with a hot cup of tea, and you will feel like fasting more often!

Preparation Time: 15 to 20 minutes
Cooking Time: 10 minutes.
Serves 4.

1 cup parboiled and grated purple yam *(kand)*
1 cup raw potatoes, peeled and grated
1 tbsp arrowroot *(paniphal)* flour
2 tsp roasted peanuts powder
2 tsp finely chopped coriander *(dhania)*
1 tsp finely chopped green chillies
Rock salt *(sendha namak)* to taste
Oil for deep-frying

For serving
Green *chutney*, page 82

1. Combine all the ingredients in a bowl and mix well.
2. Heat the oil in a non-stick *kadhai*, drop spoonfuls of the mixture in it and deep-fry on a medium flame till the *pakodas* are golden brown in colour from all the sides. Drain on absorbent paper.
   Serve hot with green *chutney*.

Handy Tip: Do not keep turning the *pakodas* frequently once immersed in oil or it may lose its shape and disintegrate.

Sabudana Wada

A very famous faraal food from the Maharashtrian repertoire, this can either be relished as a quick snack or as a whole meal along with curds and chutney!

Preparation Time: 20 minutes.
Cooking Time: 8 to 10 minutes.
Makes 8 *wadas*.
Soaking Time: 4 to 5 hours.

½ cup sago *(sabudana)*
1 cup boiled, peeled and mashed potatoes
⅓ cup roasted peanuts, coarsely crushed
½ tsp cumin seeds *(jeera)*
1 tsp grated ginger *(adrak)*
1½ tsp finely chopped green chillies
2 tbsp finely chopped coriander *(dhania)*
½ tsp lemon juice (optional)
A pinch of sugar (optional)
Rock salt *(sendha namak)* to taste
Oil for deep-frying

For serving
Green *chutney*, page 82
1 cup chilled sweetened curds *(dahi)* (1 cup fresh curds mixed with 3 tbsp powdered sugar)

1. Clean, wash and soak the sago in approx. ⅓ cup of water for about 4 to 5 hours or till all the water is absorbed and the sago swells.
2. Add all the remaining ingredients and mix well.
3. Divide the mixture into 8 equal portions and shape each portion into a 75 mm. (3") diameter flat round.
4. Heat the oil in a *kadhai* and deep-fry the *wadas* on a medium flame till they turn light brown in colour from both the sides. Drain on absorbent paper.

   Serve hot with green *chutney* and sweetened curds.

Healthy Wafer Platter

A low-calorie, anytime and all-time favourite. Let us minus the oil and make a healthy version in the microwave, so that your fasting is truly fat-free

Preparation time : 5 minutes.
Cooking time : 16 minutes.

KAND WAFERS

Makes 2 cups.

2 cups peeled and thinly sliced purple yam *(kand)*
1 tsp oil
2 tsp freshly ground pepper
Rock salt *(sendha namak)* to taste

1. Place a butter paper on a microwave safe plate and arrange ½ cup of the purple yam slices on it. Keep enough distance between the slices and do not overlap them.
2. Microwave on HIGH for 4 minutes, turning them thrice in between.
3. Grease both your hands using ¼ tsp of oil, sprinkle rock salt and ½ tsp of pepper over the *kand* wafers and toss them well with your hands.
4. Repeat with the remaining ingredients to make 3 more batches.
5. Cool completely and store in air-tight container.

BANANA PEPPER WAFERS

Makes 2 cups.

2 raw bananas, peeled and sliced
1 tsp oil
Rock salt (*sendha namak*) to taste
2 tsp freshly ground pepper

1. Place a butter paper on a microwave safe plate and arrange ½ of the raw banana slices on it. Keep enough distance between the slices and do not overlap them.
2. Microwave on HIGH for 4 minutes, turning them thrice in between.
3. Grease both your hands using ¼ tsp of oil, sprinkle rock salt and ½ tsp of pepper over the banana wafers and toss them well with your hands.
4. Repeat with the remaining ingredients to make 3 more batches.
5. Cool completely and store in air-tight container.

LOW CAL POTATO WAFERS

Makes 3 cups.

2 medium sized potatoes, peeled and sliced
1 tsp oil
Rock salt (*sendha namak*) to taste

1. Place a butter paper on a microwave safe plate and arrange ¼ of the potato slices on it. Keep enough distance between the slices and do not overlap them.
2. Microwave on HIGH for 4 minutes, turning them thrice in between.
3. Grease both your hands using ¼ tsp of oil, sprinkle rock salt over the potato wafers and toss them well with your hands.
4. Repeat with the ingredients to make 3 more batches.
5. Cool completely and store in air-tight container.

Handy Tip: Do not make the slices very thin to avoid the wafers from being partially overburnt.

Stuffed Kand Sandwich

These dainty looking sandwiches call for a little effort in cutting and cooking the purple yam pieces, but the end result is just awesome. Serve it with fresh curds or enjoy it as is.

Preparation Time: 10 minutes.
Cooking Time: 15 to 20 minutes.
Makes 10 to 12 sandwiches.

¼ kg purple yam *(kand)*
Rock salt *(sendha namak)* and freshly ground pepper to taste
10 to 12 tbsp green *chutney*, page 82
Oil for cooking

For serving
Fresh curds *(dahi)*

1. Peel and wash the purple yam and steam it in a pressure cooker for 1 whistle.
2. Allow the steam to escape before opening the lid.
3. Cut the purple yam into 50 mm. (2") x 50 mm. (2") pieces of ½ cm. width. You will get approximately 20 to 24 pieces.
4. Sprinkle a little rock salt and pepper on the purple yam pieces and toss gently.
5. Apply 1 tbsp of green *chutney* evenly on half the purple yam pieces and sandwich using the remaining pieces.
6. Heat a non-stick *tava* (griddle) and cook each *kand* sandwich, using a little oil, till they are golden brown in colour from both the sides.

Serve hot with fresh curds.

Faraali Idli-Sambhar

The famous Southie snack can be converted into a healthy and delicious faraal snack by making the idlis with sanwa millet and the sambhar with boiled vegetable purée. Serve with peanut curd chutney for an added dash of innovativeness.

Preparation Time: 20 minutes.
Cooking Time: 40 minutes.
Serves 4.
Soaking Time: 6 to 8 hours.

For the *idli*

1 cup sanwa millet *(sama)*

½ cup sago *(sabudana)*

1 cup fresh curds *(dahi)*

4 tsp ginger-green chilli paste

Rock salt *(sendha namak)* to taste

1 tsp oil

1 tsp cumin seeds *(jeera)*

1 cup boiled and peeled potato cubes

2 tsp sugar

1 tsp lemon juice

½ cup roasted peanut powder

For the *sambhar*

5 tsp coriander *(dhania)* seeds

4 round red chillies *(boriya mirch)*

2 tbsp roasted peanuts

1 tbsp grated dry coconut *(kopra)*
25 mm. (1") stick cinnamon *(dalchini)*
1½ cups bottle gourd *(lauki/ doodhi)* cubes
1½ cups peeled and chopped yam *(suran)*
1 cup peeled and chopped potatoes
Rock salt *(sendha namak)* to taste
2 tsp oil
1 tsp cumin seeds *(jeera)*
1 tsp lemon juice

For serving
Peanut curd *chutney*, page 76

For the *idli*

1. Clean and wash the *sanwa* millet and sago.
2. Drain, add the curds, 2 tsp of ginger-green chilli paste and rock salt and mix well.
3. Keep aside to soak for at least 6 to 8 hours.
4. For the stuffing, heat the oil in a non-stick *kadhai* and add the cumin seeds.
5. When the seeds crackle, add the remaining 2 tsp of ginger-green chilli paste and sauté on a medium flame for a few seconds.
6. Add the potatoes, sugar, lemon juice and rock salt, mix well and cook on a slow flame for 5 minutes.
7. Cool and divide the stuffing into 16 equal portions.
8. Put 1 tbsp of the *idli* batter into greased *idli* moulds, spread a portion of the potato stuffing and sprinkle a little peanut powder over it and finely top it up with another tbsp of the *idli* batter.

9. Repeat with the remaining batter to make 15 more *idlis*.
10. Steam in an *idli* steamer for 10 minutes or till done.

For the *sambhar*

1. Combine the coriander seeds, 2 round red chillies, peanuts, dry coconut and cinnamon and blend in a mixer to a fine powder. Keep aside.
2. Boil a vesselful of water, add 1 cup of bottle gourd, 1 cup of yam and potatoes and cook for 8 to 10 minutes or till the vegetables are completely cooked.
3. Drain, cool and blend in a mixer to a smooth purée.
4. Transfer it to a deep non-stick pan, add 4 cups of water, mix well and simmer for 7 to 8 minutes, while stirring once in between.
5. Add the remaining ½ cup of bottle gourd and yam, ground powder and rock salt, mix well and cook for 3 to 4 minutes.
6. For the tempering, heat the oil in a small non-stick pan and add the cumin seeds.
7. When the seeds crackle, add the remaining 2 round red chillies and sauté on a slow flame for a few seconds.
8. Pour the tempering over the boiling *sambhar*, mix well and simmer for another 3 to 4 minutes.
9. Add the lemon juice and mix well.

How to serve

Serve hot *idlis* with *sambhar* and peanut curd *chutney*.

Khandvi

Khandvi, one of the gems of Gujarati cuisine, has been modified into faraali style, so that it can be enjoyed as a light snack on fasting days.

Preparation Time: 10 minutes.
Cooking Time: 10 minutes.
Serves 4.

1 cup arrowroot *(paniphal)* flour
¼ cup *rajgira* flour
2 tsp ginger-green chilli paste
Rock salt *(sendha namak)* to taste
1 cup curds *(dahi)*
¼ tsp oil for greasing
1 tbsp oil
1 tsp cumin seeds *(jeera)*
1 tsp sesame seeds *(til)*
5 to 6 curry leaves *(kadi patta)*

For the garnish
2 tbsp finely chopped coriander *(dhania)*
2 tbsp freshly grated coconut, optional

For serving
Green *chutney*, page 82

1. Combine the arrowroot flour, *rajgira* flour, ginger-green chilli paste, rock salt, curds and 1½ cups of water together in a deep non-stick pan and mix well, taking care no lump remains.
2. Cook on a slow flame, while stirring continuously, till the mixture becomes thick (approx. 8 to 10 minutes).
3. Spread a spoonful of the batter on the reverse side of a greased *thali* and wait for a few seconds and try to roll up. If it doesn't then cook for few more minutes and try once more to roll up.
4. Divide the batter into 2 equal portions.
5. Spread each portion on the reverse side of 2 greased *thalis* (approximately 10" in diameter) evenly to make a thin uniform layer using a spatula, while the mixture is still hot.
6. When cool, make cuts at a distance of 1½" to 2" lengthwise on each *thali* and roll it up gently. Place the *khandvis* on a serving plate.
7. For the tempering, heat the oil in a small non-stick pan and add the cumin seeds.
8. When the seeds crackle, add the sesame seeds and curry leaves and sauté on a medium flame for a few seconds.
9. Pour the tempering over the *khandvis*.
   Garnish with coconut and coriander and serve with green *chutney*.

Sanwa Panki

This unique panki recipe gets its delicate flavour after being cooked between banana leaves. Green chutney is a great combo for this delectable dish.

Preparation Time: 15 minutes.
Cooking Time: 20 minutes.
Makes approx. 15 *pankis*.
Fermenting Time: 1 hour.

2 cups sanwa millet *(sama)*, ground into a fine powder
½ cup *rajgira* flour
4 tbsp arrowroot *(paniphal)* flour
2 tbsp *ghee*
1 tsp cumin seeds *(jeera)*
¾ cup sour curds *(khatta dahi)*, beaten
Rock salt *(sendha namak)* to taste
1 tbsp finely chopped coriander *(dhania)*
1½ tsp ginger-green chilli paste
4 to 6 banana leaves, cut into 150 mm. x 150 mm. (6" x 6") square pieces
Oil for greasing and cooking

For serving
Green *chutney*, page 82
Bhavanagari chillies, page 80

1. Blend the sanwa millet in a mixer to a fine powder and keep aside.

2. Transfer it to a bowl, add the *rajgira* and arrowroot flours, curds, rock salt, coriander, ginger-green chilli paste, cumin seeds and ½ cup of water in a bowl and mix well to make a batter of pouring consistency. Cover and keep aside to ferment for 1 hour.

3. Grease one side of each banana leaf with a little oil and keep aside.

4. Pour 2 tbsp of the batter on one half of the greased side of a banana leaf and spread it evenly to make a thin layer.

5. Fold the other side of the banana leaf over the batter.

6. Heat on a non-stick pan or a *tava* (griddle) and cook it on a medium flame, using a little oil, till light brown spots appear on both the sides of the leaves and the *panki* peels off the leaf easily.

7. Repeat with the remaining ingredients to make 14 more *pankis*.

Serve immediately with green *chutney* and Bhavnagari chillies.

Layered Handva

Tempting paneer teamed with spicy green chutney is sandwiched between purple yam and potato and baked to perfection.

Preparation Time : 20 to 25 minutes.
Cooking Time: Nil. Serves 4.
Baking time : 200°C (400°F).
Baking time : 25 minutes.

To be mixed into *kand* mixture

1 cup peeled, parboiled and grated purple yam *(kand)*

1 tsp finely chopped green chillies

2 tsp sugar

1 tsp lemon juice

1 tbsp arrowroot *(paniphal)* flour

Rock salt *(sendha namak)* to taste

To be mixed into *paneer* mixture

1 cup thickly grated *paneer* (cottage cheese), page 94

¼ cup green *chutney*, page 82

Rock salt *(sendha namak)* to taste

To be mixed into potato mixture

1 cup peeled, parboiled and grated potatoes

1 tsp finely chopped green chillies

2 tsp sugar
1 tsp lemon juice
1 tbsp arrowroot *(paniphal)* flour
Rock salt *(sendha namak)* to taste

Other ingredients
½ tsp ghee for greasing
1 tbsp oil
½ tsp cumin seeds *(jeera)*
1 tbsp sesame seeds *(til)*

For serving
Peanut curd *chutney*, page 76
Green *chutney*, page 82

1. Grease the baking dish using ½ tsp of ghee.
2. Spread the *kand* mixture evenly at the bottom of a greased baking dish, followed by the *paneer* mixture and finally the potato mixture. Keep aside.
3. Heat the oil in a small non-stick *kadhai* and add the cumin seeds.
4. When the seeds crackle, add the sesame seeds and sauté for a few seconds.
5. Pour this tempering over the layered baking dish and bake in a pre-heated oven at 200°C (400°F) for 20 minutes or till light brown in colour. Keep aside to cool.
6. Cut into 8 equal pieces and serve hot with peanut curd *chutney* and green *chutney*.

Faraali Pattice

Available in the shops and streets of Mumbai, this famous pattice is made with a crunchy peanut and coconut stuffing.

Preparation Time: 15 to 20 minutes.
Cooking Time: 10 to 12 minutes.
Makes 8 *pattice*.

To be mixed together into a potato mixture

1¾ cups boiled, peeled and mashed potatoes

3 tbsp arrowroot *(paniphal)* flour

Rock salt *(sendha namak)* to taste

To be mixed together into a stuffing

⅓ cup freshly grated coconut

3 tbsp peanuts, roasted and powdered

3 tbsp finely chopped coriander *(dhania)*

1½ tsp chopped raisins *(kismis)*

1½ tsp chopped cashewnuts *(kaju)*

1 tbsp ginger-green chilli paste

1½ tbsp sugar

1 tbsp of lemon juice

Rock salt *(sendha namak)* to taste

Other ingredients

Arrowroot *(paniphal)* flour for coating
Oil for deep-frying

For serving

Sweetened curds, page 25
Green *chutney*, page 82

1. Divide the potato mixture and the stuffing both into 8 equal portions and keep aside.
2. Flatten a portion of the potato mixture into a 75 mm. (3") diameter circle and place a portion of the stuffing in the centre.
3. Bring together the edges in the centre to seal the stuffing and shape it into a round ball. Keep aside.
4. Repeat with the remaining potato mixture and stuffing to make 7 more *pattice*.
5. Roll the *pattice* in the arrowroot flour till they are evenly coated from all the sides.
6. Heat the oil in a *kadhai* and deep-fry the *pattice* on a medium flame till they turn brown in colour from all the sides. Drain on absorbent paper.

   Serve immediately with sweetened curds and green *chutney*.

Faraali Pahadi Tikka

An exotic recipe made using the traditional upvaas ingredients – potatoes, kand, shakark and and paneer with the flavourful minty marinade as an elegant touch.

Preparation Time: 25 minutes.
Cooking Time: 15 to 20 minutes.
Makes 8 to 10 *tikkas*.

To be ground into a smooth green marinade

½ cup fresh hung curds *(dahi),* refer handy tip

1½ cups chopped mint leaves *(phudina)*

1 cup chopped coriander *(dhania)*

2 tsp cumin seeds *(jeera)*

2 tbsp chopped green chillies

2 tsp lemon juice

Rock salt *(sendha namak)* to taste

Other ingredients

2 cups *paneer* (cottage cheese), page 94, cut into 25 mm. (1") cubes

1 cup baby potatoes, peeled, cut into halves and parboiled

1 cup sweet potato *(shakarkand)* peeled, cut into 25 mm. (1") slices and parboiled

1 cup purple yam *(kand)*, peeled, cut into 25 mm. (1") cubes and parboiled

1 tbsp oil

1. Thread one piece each of the *paneer*, purple yam, sweet potato and baby potato halves onto a toothpick. Repeat with the remaining ingredients to make more *tikkas*.
2. Apply the green marinade evenly on the *paneer* and the vegetables and keep aside for 15 to 20 minutes.
3. Heat a non-stick *tava* (griddle) and cook the *tikkas* on a medium flame, using a little oil, till the *paneer* and vegetables are light brown in colour from all the sides.
   Serve immediately.

Handy tip: 1 cup of curds when tied in a muslin cloth and hanged for ½ hour gives ½ cup of hung curds.

Upvaas Thalipeeth

Giving an interesting twist to the regular Maharashtrian thalipeeth, I have made it with a combination of rajgira flour and grated potatoes. Serve it with green chutney and fresh curds for a light and healthy meal.

Preparation Time: 15 minutes.
Cooking Time: 10 minutes.
Makes 4 *thalipeeths*.

½ cup *rajgira* flour
¼ cup peeled and grated raw potatoes
2 tbsp roasted peanut powder
Rock salt *(sendha namak)* to taste
½ tsp lemon juice
2 tbsp chopped coriander *(dhania)*
1 tsp green chilli paste
Ghee for greasing and cooking

For serving
Fresh curds *(dahi)*
Green *chutney*, page 82

1. Combine all the ingredients along with 2 tsp of water in a bowl and mix well to make a thick batter.
2. Divide the batter into 4 equal portions and keep aside.
3. Heat a non-stick pan and grease it lightly with ghee.

1. Wet your fingers and spread a portion of the batter with it on the *tava* (griddle) to form a 100 mm. (4") diameter thick circle.
2. Cook, using a little *ghee*, till they turn golden brown in colour on both the sides.
3. Repeat with the remaining batter to make 3 more *thalipeeths*.
   Serve hot with fresh curds and green *chutney*.

Rajgira Paneer Paratha

These paneer stuffed parathas are a meal in their own right. Remember not to give too much force when patting the parathas to ensure that they do not break.

Preparation Time: 10 to 15 minutes.
Cooking Time : 20 minutes.
Makes 6 *parathas*.

To be mixed into a stuffing

1 cup thickly grated fresh *paneer* (cottage cheese), page 94
2 tsp finely chopped green chillies
½ tsp lemon juice
½ tsp sugar
2 tsp finely chopped coriander *(dhania)*
Rock salt *(sendha namak)* to taste

Other ingredients

1 cup *rajgira* flour
¼ cup boiled, peeled and mashed potatoes
½ tsp black pepper powder
Rock salt *(sendha namak)* to taste
Rajgira flour for rolling
Oil for cooking

For serving
Green *chutney*, page 82
Fresh curds *(dahi)*

1. Divide the stuffing into 6 equal portions and keep aside.
2. Combine the *rajgira* flour, potatoes, pepper powder and rock salt in a bowl and knead into a semi-soft dough using enough water.
3. Divide the dough into 6 equal portions and roll out a portion into a 75 mm. (3") diameter circle, using a little *rajgira* flour for rolling.
4. Place a portion of the stuffing in the centre of the circle, bring the edges in the centre and seal tightly.
5. Roll out again into a 150 mm. (6") diameter circle, using a little *rajgira* flour for rolling.
6. Heat a non-stick *tava* (griddle) and cook the *paratha*, using a little oil, till it turns golden brown in colour from both the sides.
7. Repeat with the remaining dough and stuffing to make 5 more *parathas*.
   Serve hot with green *chutney* and fresh curds.

Minty Sanwa

A normal khichdi recipe when flavoured with coconut milk, coriander and mint, morphs into an interesting Thai style sanwa. Serve hot, immediately, with lemon wedges for an extra zing.

Preparation Time ; 15 to 20 minutes.
Cooking Time : 15 minutes.
Serves 4.
Soaking Time : 1 hour.

1½ cups sanwa millet *(sama)*
2 tbsp oil
3 cups coconut milk *(nariyal ka doodh)*
Rock salt *(sendha namak)* to taste
4 tbsp chopped coriander *(dhania)*
4 tbsp chopped fresh mint leaves *(phudina)*
½ tbsp finely chopped green chillies

For serving
4 lemon wedges
Peanut Kadhi, page 63 / Yam Raita, page 78

1. Clean, wash and soak the sanwa millet in enough water for 1 hour. Drain well and keep aside.
2. Heat the oil in a deep non-stick pan, add the sanwa millet and sauté on a medium flame for 4 to 5 minutes.
3. Add the coconut milk, ½ cup of water and rock salt and mix well.
4. Cover and cook on a slow flame, while stirring occasionally, till all the liquid is absorbed and the sanwa millet is cooked. Add a little water if required.

5. Add the coriander, mint leaves and green chillies and mix well.
   Serve hot garnished with lemon wedges and peanut *kadhi* / yam *raita*.

Dahiwali Aloo ki Subzi with Rajgira Puri

This potato-based dish comprises all the spices that are allowed during fasts, assembled in a manner to please the choosiest of connoisseurs. Enjoy it with rajgira puris.

Preparation Time : 20 to 25 minutes.
Cooking Time : 20 to 25 minutes.
Serves 4.

For the *aloo subzi*

1 cup fresh curds *(dahi)*, beaten
½ tsp arrowroot *(paniphal)* flour
1 tbsp *ghee*
½ tsp cumin seeds *(jeera)*
1 bayleaf *(tejpatta)*
2 cloves *(laung / lavang)*
25 mm (1") stick cinnamon *(dalchini)*
1 tsp round red chilli *(boriya mirch)* powder, refer handy tip
1 tsp coriander-cumin seed *(dhania-jeera)* powder
12-15 baby potatoes, boiled and peeled
Rock salt *(sendha namak)* to taste
2 tbsp finely chopped coriander *(dhania)*

For the *rajgira puris*

1 cup *rajgira* flour
½ cup boiled, peeled and mashed potatoes
2 tbsp arrowroot *(paniphal)* flour
1 tbsp hot melted ghee
Rock salt *(sendha namak)* to taste
Ghee for deep-frying

For the *aloo subzi*

1. Combine the curds and arrowroot flour in a bowl, mix well and keep aside.
2. Heat the ghee in a *kadhai* and add the cumin seeds.
3. When they crackle, add the bayleaf, cloves and cinnamon and sauté on a medium flame for a few seconds.
4. Add the curds mixture, round red chilli powder and coriander-cumin seed powder, mix well and cook on medium flame for 3 to 4 minutes, while stirring continuously.
5. Add the baby potatoes, rock salt and ½ cup of water, mix well and cook on a medium flame for another 6 to 7 minutes. Top with coriander and keep aside.

For the *rajgira puris*

1. Combine all the ingredients together in a bowl and knead into a semi-stiff dough using enough water.
2. Divide the dough into 16 equal portions and roll each portion into a 75 mm. (3") diameter circle.
3. Heat the ghee in a *kadhai* and deep-fry the *puris*, a few at a time, till they turn golden brown in colour from both the sides.

For serving

Serve hot *rajgira puris* with hot *aloo subzi*.

Handy tip : To make round red chilli powder, dry roast 2 to 3 whole round red chillis (*boriya mirch*) on a *tava* (griddle) for 2 to 3 minutes. Cool slightly, deseed and blend it in a mixer to a fine powder. Use as required.

Peanut Kadhi

An ingenious kadhi recipe flavoured with peanuts and cumin seeds, this is a wonderful match for Buckwheat Khichdi / Minty Sanwa etc.

Preparation Time : 5 to 7 minutes.
Cooking Time : 7 to 8 minutes.
Serves 4.

1 cup fresh curds *(dahi)*
1 tbsp *rajgira* flour
1 tsp ghee
1 tsp cumin seeds *(jeera)*
1 tbsp ginger-green chilli paste
2 tbsp roasted peanut powder
Rock salt *(sendha namak)* to taste
½ tsp sugar

For the garnish
1 tsp finely chopped coriander *(dhania)*

For serving
Minty Sanwa, page 57 / Buckwheat *Khichdi*, page 71

1. Combine the curds, *rajgira* flour and 2 cups of water in a bowl and whisk well. Keep aside.
2. Heat the ghee in a deep non-stick pan and add the cumin seeds.

3. When the seeds crackle, add the ginger–green chilli paste and sauté on a medium flame for 30 seconds.
4. Add the roasted peanut powder and sauté on a medium flame for another 30 seconds.
5. Add the curds-rajgira flour mixture, rock salt and sugar, mix well and cook on a slow flame for 4 to 5 minutes, while stirring continuously to avoid any lump formation.

Garnish with coriander and serve hot with minty sanwa / buckwheat *khichdi*.

Faraali Misal

The humble sabudana khichdi transforms into an interesting misal eligible for a fasting day, when topped with a peanut-potato mixture and faraali chivda.

Preparation Time : 10 to 15 minutes.
Cooking Time : 15 to 20 minutes.
Serves 4.
Soaking Time : 4 hours.

For the *sabudana khichdi*

1 cup sago *(sabudana)*
1 tbsp ghee
1 tsp cumin seeds *(jeera)*
1 tbsp ginger-green chilli paste
¼ cup roasted and coarsely crushed peanuts
Rock salt *(sendha namak)* to taste
1 tsp lemon juice

For the potato peanut mixture

5 round red chillies *(boriya mirch)*, dry roasted and powdered
1 tsp whole coriander *(dhania)* seeds, dry roasted and powdered
2 tsp oil
1 tsp cumin seeds *(jeera)*
1½ cups medium sized potatoes, unpeeled and cut into 25 mm. (1 ") cubes
3 tbsp peanuts, soaked for 1 hour and drained

67

3 *kokum*, soaked for 1 hour and drained
Rock salt *(sendha namak)* to taste

Other ingredients
4 tbsp *faraali chivda*, readily available in the market
Lemon wedges

For the garnish
2 tbsp chopped coriander *(dhania)*

For the *sabudana khichdi*
1. Clean, wash and soak the sago in enough water for at least 4 hours. Drain, spread on a *thali* and keep aside to dry for 1 hour.
2. Heat the ghee in a deep non-stick pan and add the cumin seeds.
3. When the seeds crackle, add the ginger-green chilli paste and sauté on a medium flame for 30 seconds.
4. Add the peanuts powder and sauté on a slow flame for another 30 seconds.
5. Add the sago and rock salt and cook on a slow flame for 4 to 5 minutes, while stirring continuously. Each grain of sago should be separate.
6. Add the lemon juice, mix well and cook on a slow flame for another 2 minutes.
7. Divide it into 4 equal portions and keep aside.

For the potato peanut mixture

1. Combine the round red chillies and coriander seeds and dry roast it on a *tava* (griddle) till they release a pleasant aroma.
2. Cool slightly and coarsely crush it using a mortar-pestle *(khalbhatta)*.
3. Heat the oil in a deep pan and add the cumin seeds and crushed chilli-coriander mixture and sauté on a medium flame for 2 to 3 minutes.
4. Add the potatoes and sauté on a medium flame for 4 to 5 minutes.
5. Add the peanuts, *kokum*, rock salt and 2 cups of water and cook till the potatoes are completely cooked.
6. Mash the potatoes slightly using the back of a spoon.
7. Divide it into 4 equal portions and keep aside.

How to serve

1. Place a portion of the *sabudana khichdi* at the base of a bowl.
2. Top with a portion of the potato peanut mixture and 1 tbsp of *faraali chivda*.
   Garnish with coriander and serve immediately with lemon wedges.

Buckwheat Khichdi

A look at this recipe and you know that fasts do not mean staying hungry! Team this khichdi with Peanut Kadhi to make a satiating meal.

Preparation Time: 10 minutes.
Cooking Time: 15 to 20 minutes.
Serves 4.
Soaking Time: 2 hours.

1 cup buckwheat *(kutto / kutti no daro)*
½ cup sour curds *(khatta dahi)*
1 tbsp oil
1 tsp cumin seeds *(jeera)*
½ cup potatoes, peeled and cut into 12 mm. (½") cubes
1 tbsp ginger-green chilli paste
2 tbsp coarsely powdered peanuts
1 tsp sugar
½ tsp lemon juice
Rock salt *(sendha namak)* to taste

For the garnish
1 tbsp chopped coriander *(dhania)*
1 tsp toasted sesame seeds *(til)*

For serving
Peanut *Kadhi*, page 63

1. Clean, wash and soak the buckwheat in enough water for 2 hours. Drain and keep aside.
2. Combine the curds with 1½ cups of water in a bowl and mix well. Keep aside.
3. Heat the oil in a deep non-stick pan and add cumin seeds.
4. When the seeds crackle, add the potatoes, mix well and cook on a medium flame till the potatoes are half-cooked.
5. Add the ginger-green chilli paste and powdered peanuts and cook, while stirring continuously, till the peanut powder turns light brown in colour and starts leaving a pleasant aroma.
6. Add the curds mixture, rock salt and buckwheat and mix well.
7. Cook on slow flame for approx. 10 to 12 minutes or till the buckwheat is cooked and the water gets evaporated, while stirring occasionally in between.

    Garnish with coriander and sesame seeds and serve hot with peanut *kadhi*.

Faraali Dosa

Here is another famous South Indian delicacy to please your palate on a fasting day. Best enjoyed with green chutney or peanut and curd chutney.

Preparation Time : 5 to 7 minutes.
Cooking Time: 5 to 7 minutes.
Makes 8 *dosas*.
Soaking Time: 2 hours.
Fermenting Time : Overnight.

½ cup sanwa millet *(sama)*
½ cup *rajgira* flour
½ cup sour buttermilk
1 tbsp ginger-green chilli paste
Rock salt *(sendha namak)* to taste
Oil for cooking

For serving

Peanut curd *chutney*, page 76 / Green *chutney*, page 82

1. Clean, wash and soak the sanwa millet in enough water for atleast 2 hours.
2. Drain and blend in a mixer to a fine paste using 2 tbsp of water.
3. Transfer the mixture to a bowl, add the *rajgira* flour, buttermilk, ginger-green chilli paste and rock salt and mix well. Cover and keep aside to ferment overnight.
4. Divide the batter into 8 equal portions and keep aside.
5. Heat a non-stick *tava* (griddle), pour a portion of the batter on the *tava* (griddle) and spread it in a circular motion to make a 125 mm. (5") diameter thin *dosa*.

6. Smear a little oil along the sides, cook till both the sides turn golden brown in colour and fold over to make a semi-circle or a triangle.

7. Repeat with the remaining batter to make 7 more *dosas*.

    Serve hot with peanut curd *chutney* or green *chutney*.

ACCOMPNIMENTS
Peanut Curd Chutney

When peanuts and fresh curds do a tango on stage, what you get is a spicy, crunchy and tangy accompaniment that goes well with Faraali Idli, page 33, Faraali Dosa, page 73, etc.

Preparation Time: 5 minutes.
Cooking Time: Nil.
Makes 1 cup.

1 cup roasted and coarsely powdered peanuts

¾ cup fresh curds *(dahi)*

1½ tsp ginger-green chilli paste

1 tbsp sugar

½ tbsp lemon juice

Rock salt *(sendha namak)* to taste

1. Combine all the ingredients and blend in a mixer till smooth.
2. Store refrigerated in an air-tight container and use as required.

Yam Raita

Think beyond the traditional ingredient cucumber when making raita on fasting days. How about using boiled and mashed yam? You are sure to love this unconventional accompaniment.

Preparation Time: 10 minutes.
Cooking Time: Nil.
Makes 1½ cups.

1 cup peeled, boiled and mashed yam *(suran)*
1 cup fresh curds *(dahi)*
Rock salt *(sendha namak)* to taste
1½ tsp sugar
½ tsp green chilli paste
½ tsp black pepper *(kalimirch)* powder
2 tsp chopped coriander *(dhania)*

1. Combine all the ingredients in a bowl and mix well.
2. Refrigerate for at least 1 hour.
   Serve chilled.

Bhavanagari Chillies

This evergreen favourite is made of Bhavanagari chillies, flavoured with sesame seeds and cumin seeds. Besan is replaced with waterchestnut flour, to make this accompaniment qualify for a fast.

Preparation Time: 5 minutes.
Cooking Time: 7 to 8 minutes.
Serves 4.

2 tbsp oil
½ tsp sesame seeds *(til)*
½ tsp cumin seeds *(jeera)*
2 tbsp waterchestnut *(shingada)* flour
1 cup sliced *Bhavanagari* chillies
½ tbsp lemon juice
Rock salt *(sendha namak)* to taste

1. Heat the oil in a non-stick *kadhai* and add the sesame seeds and cumin seeds.
2. When the seeds crackle, add the waterchestnut flour and cook on a slow flame for 2 to 3 minutes, while stirring continuously, till the flour is cooked.
3. Add the *Bhavanagari* chillies, lemon juice and rock salt and cook on a slow flame for 5 minutes, stirring once in between.
   Serve immediately.

Handy tip: If refrigerated, it stays fresh for 2 to 3 days, but remember to re-heat before serving.

Green Chutney

This tangy and tongue-tickling chutney can be enjoyed with anything you eat during a fast – be it a snack or a meal.

Preparation Time: 10 minutes.
Cooking Time: Nil.
Makes 1 cup.

1½ cups chopped coriander (*dhania*)
4 green chillies, roughly chopped
4 tbsp grated coconut
1½ tsp lemon juice
2 tsp sugar
Rock salt (*sendha namak*) to taste

1. Combine all the ingredients and blend in a mixer till smooth.
2. Store refrigerated in an air-tight container and use as required.

Khaman Kakdi

An accompaniment can make or break a meal. A well-planned accompaniment can make even a simple meal glow. Here is something to go with your meals on fasting days.

Preparation Time: 10 minutes.
Cooking Time: A few minutes.
Serves 4.

2 tsp oil
1 tsp sesame seeds *(til)*
1 tsp cumin seeds *(jeera)*
½ cup coarsely crushed roasted peanuts
1½ cups cucumber cubes
2 tbsp chopped coriander *(dhania)*
½ tbsp lemon juice
A pinch sugar
Rock salt *(sendha namak)* to taste

1. Heat the oil in a *kadhai* and add the sesame seeds and cumin seeds.
2. When they crackle, add the peanuts and rock salt and sauté on a medium flame for a minute.
3. Add the cucumber and coriander and mix well.
4. Just before serving, add the lemon juice, sugar and rock salt and mix well.
   Serve immediately.

DESSERTS
Sweet Faraali Pancakes

A delectable meal deserves a sweet finish. So, say goodbye to the dining table with these banana and coconut flavoured pancakes.

Preparation Time: 10 minutes.
Cooking Time: 20 minutes.
Makes approx. 18 to 20 pancakes.
Soaking Time : 1 hour.

1 cup sanwa millet *(sama)*
½ cup buckwheat *(kutto / kutti no daro)*
1 cup grated coconut
½ cup grated jaggery *(gur)*
½ cup mashed banana

A pinch of rock salt *(sendha namak)*
¼ tsp cardamom *(elaichi)* powder
Ghee for cooking

For serving
Sweetened curds, page 25

1. Clean, wash and soak the sanwa millet and buckwheat separately in enough water for atleast 1 hour. Drain and keep aside

2. Blend the sanwa millet and buckwheat separately by adding 2 tbsp of water in a mixer to a fine paste.

3. Combine the sanwa paste, buckwheat paste, coconut, jaggery, banana, rock salt and cardamom powder in a bowl and mix well.

4. Heat a non-stick *tava* (griddle), pour a ladleful of the batter and spread it in a circular motion to make a 75 mm. (3") diameter thin pancake.

5. Cook, using a little ghee, till it turns golden brown in colour from both the sides.

6. Repeat with the remaining batter to make 14 more pancakes.
   Serve hot with sweetened curds.

Shakarkand ka Halwa

An irresistibly sweet dish made from a sweet ingredient! Try this unique halwa recipe made using sweet potatoes, flavoured with cardamom powder and saffron, and enriched with nuts to keep your energy levels high.

Preparation Time: 10 minutes.
Cooking Time: 12 to 15 minutes.
Serves 4.

3 medium sized sweet potatoes *(shakarkand)*

1 tsp ghee

¾ cup milk

4 tbsp sugar

¼ tsp cardamom *(elaichi)* powder

A few saffron strands *(kesar)* dissolved in 1 tbsp milk

2 tbsp chopped mixed nuts (almonds, cashewnuts, pistachios etc.)

1. Clean and wash sweet potatoes and pressure cook for 3 to 4 whistles. Allow the steam to escape before opening.
2. Peel and mash the sweet potatoes and keep aside.
3. Heat the ghee in a non-stick pan, add the mashed sweet potatoes and sauté on a medium flame for 2 to 3 minutes.
4. Add the milk, ½ cup of water, sugar and cardamom powder, mix well and simmer for 1 to 2 minutes, ensuring that the mixture has little liquid remaining and not completely dry.
5. Add the saffron and mixed nuts and mix well.
   Serve hot.

Paneer Kheer

A wholesome kheer recipe, elegantly laced with the sweet flavour of cardamom and topped with mixed nuts.

Preparation Time: 10 minutes.
Cooking Time: 15 to 17 minutes.
Serves 4.

1½ cups milk
½ cup grated *paneer* (cottage cheese), page 94
1¼ cups condensed milk
½ tsp cardamom *(elaichi)* powder
3 tbsp chopped mixed nuts (cashewnuts, almonds and pistachios)

For the garnish

1 tbsp almond *(badam)* and pistachio slivers

1. Combine the milk and *paneer* in a broad non-stick pan and bring to boil, while stirring continuously.
2. Simmer for 5 to 7 minutes, while stirring continuously.
3. Add the condensed milk and simmer for another 4 to 5 minutes.
4. Remove from the flame, add the cardamom powder and mixed nuts and mix well.
5. Refrigerate for at least 1 hour.
   Serve chilled garnished with almonds and pistachios.

Singhada Sheera

A pleasant recipe to woo your sweet tooth, this sheera of waterchestnut flour is definitely worth a try.

Preparation Time: 10 minutes.
Cooking Time: 15 to 20 minutes.
Serves 4.

4 tbsp ghee
1 cup waterchestnut *(singhada)* flour
¾ cup sugar
½ tsp cardamom *(elaichi)* powder

For the garnish
1 tbsp almond *(badam)* slivers
1 tbsp pistachio slivers

1. Heat the ghee in a broad non-stick pan, add the waterchestnut flour and cook on a slow flame for 3 to 5 minutes or till it becomes golden brown in colour, while stirring continuously.
2. Add 2 cups of warm water, mix well and cook on a medium flame for 8 to 10 minutes or till all the water is absorbed, while stirring continuously.
3. Add the sugar, mix well and cook on a medium flame for another 5 to 7 minutes or till the ghee separates.
4. Add the cardamom powder and mix well.
   Serve hot garnished with almonds and pistachios.

BASIC RECIPE
Paneer

The Indian answer to ricotta cheese! Learn to master the art of making the perfect paneer at home to ensure fresh paneer each time. It has high moisture content and is best refrigerated when not in use. The best way to do this would be to store it in a bowl filled with cold water and use it within 3 days. Don't forget to change the water everyday.

Preparation Time: Nil.
Cooking Time: 10 minutes.
Makes approx. 1 cup.

1 litre full fat milk
2 tsp lemon juice

1. Put the milk to boil. When it starts boiling, remove from the flame and wait for a while.
2. Add the lemon juice and stir gently. When it curdles, strain using a muslin cloth. Let the whey drain out and use the *paneer* as required.
3. If you want solid *paneer*, put some weight on the drained *paneer* and leave it on for some time. Cut into desired pieces and use as required.

Handy tip: You can also use 1½ tsp vinegar or 1½ tsp citric acid crystals instead of 2 tsp of lemon juice for curdling the milk.

Latest in Mini Series
by *Tarla Dalal*

100 calorie Snacks

Paneer Snacks

Pressure Cooker Recipes

Popular Restaurant Gravies

Protein Rich Recipes

Know Your Green Leafy Vegetables

Know your Flours

Know your Spices

Know your Dals & Pulses

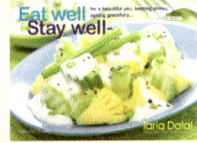

Eat well Stay well